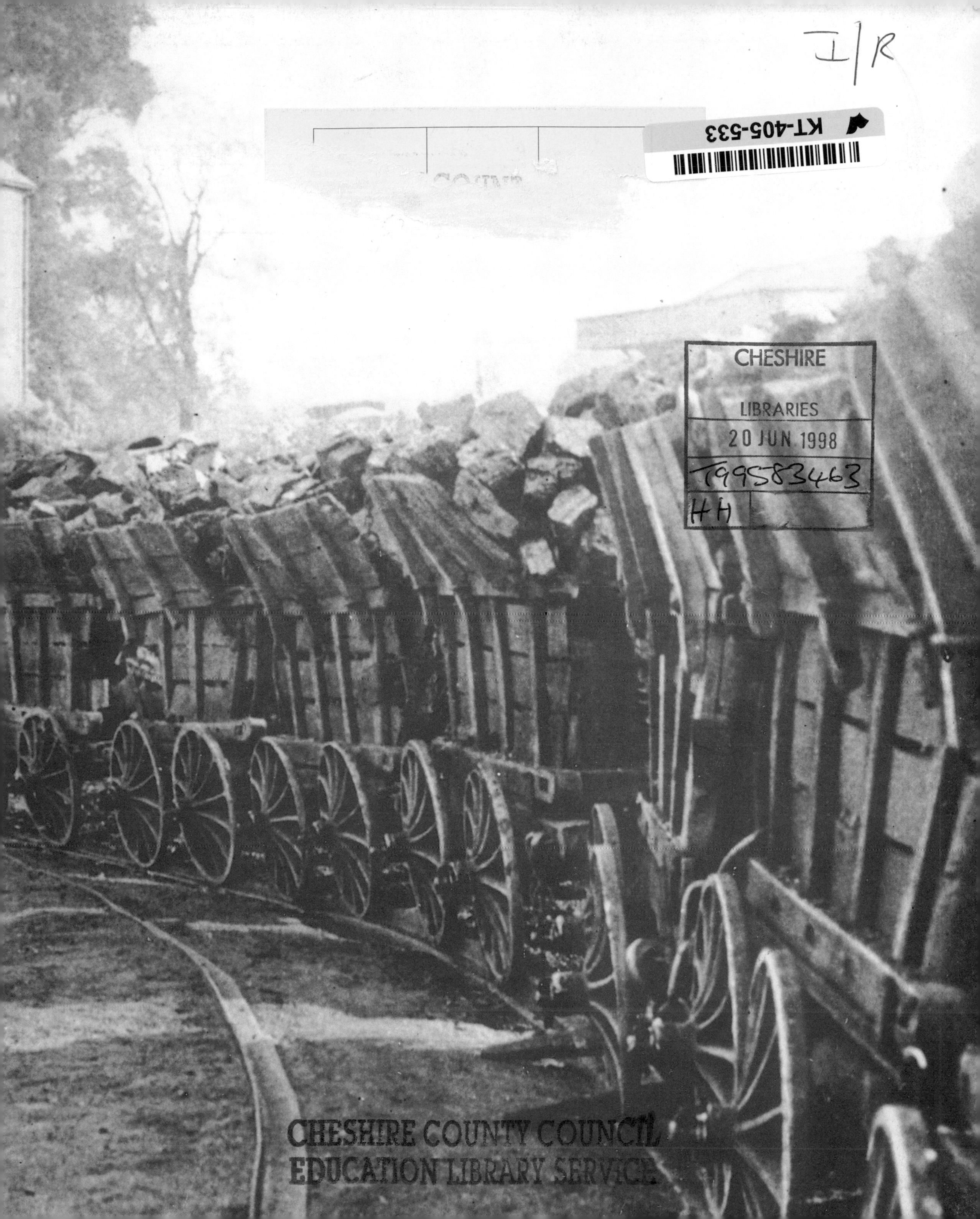

Children of

Cover pictures: (main picture) *The Foundry* by Eyre Crowe
(1824–1910); (small pictures) drawings from 1842 showing how coal
was moved underground.
Inside cover picture: Horses pulling carts of coal along a wagon-way.
Above: The Dalmellington Ironworks in Ayrshire in 1903. Workers'
housing can be seen to the left of the picture, overlooked by the
general manager's house on the hill. The drawing beneath the
photograph shows a coal bearer and comes from the Coal
Commission Report of 1842.

First published in 1996 by Wayland (Publishers) Ltd,
61 Western Road, Hove, East Sussex BN3 1JD, England.
© Copyright 1996 Wayland (Publishers) Ltd.

British Library Cataloguing in Publication Data
Rose, Iain
    Children of Coal and Iron
    I. Title II. MacLean, Donald
    331.382233409411

ISBN 0-7502-1789-8

Editor: Katrina Maitland Smith
Consultant: Donald Gunn, Education Officer for BBC Education
Scotland
Picture researcher: Elizabeth Miller
Concept design: Derek Lee
Book design and typesetting: Pardoe Blacker Ltd
Printed and bound by B.P.C. Paulton Books Ltd

The right of Iain Rose and Donald MacLean to be identified as the
Authors of this work has been asserted in accordance with the
Copyright, Designs and Patents Act 1988 Sections 77 and 78.

Picture acknowledgements
The publishers would like to thank the following for providing the illustrations for this book: The Bridgeman Art Library *main cover picture* (Forbes Magazine
Collection, New York), 22; Central Region Archives, Scotland 26, 27; Dalmellington and District Conservation Trust *imprint/contents page*, 30; Mary Evans
13 (bottom), 16, 23, 34, 35 (top); Hulton Deutsch Collection 20-21, 24, 37; by kind permission of the Keeper of the Records of Scotland 17 (bottom); National
Galleries of Scotland 31, 36; Panos Pictures 40 (Jim Holmes), 41 (Hugh O'Shaughnessy); Ann Ronan at Image Select 10 (left), 11 (top), 12, 18, 19, 28-9, 32;
The Science Museum/Science & Society Picture Library 15 (top); Tony Stone 35 (bottom); The Trustees of the National Library of Scotland 8 (top), 9 (both), 10
(right), 11 (bottom), 38; Wayland *cover* (top, both), *inside cover picture* and 14 (© National Railway Museum).
Maps and artwork by Hardlines: 6, 7, 8 (bottom), 13 (top), 15 (bottom), 17 (top), 25, 33, 39. Map on page 43 by Sallie Alane Reason, with labels by Hardlines.

Coal and Iron

Contents

Coal

Millions of years ago, Scotland was covered with thick forests. When the trees and plants died and fell, mud and sand covered them over. More trees and plants grew and, when they died, they were also covered by mud and sand. This happened over and over again.

Over thousands of years, these trees and plants turned into coal. The mud and sand became shale and sandstone. Coal, therefore, is found in layers which are called seams.

WHERE COAL WAS FOUND IN SCOTLAND

Coal has been mined in Scotland for hundreds of years. At first, it was found lying on the ground where the coal-seam was very near to the surface. Later, as more coal was needed, people, called miners, began to dig pits into the earth looking for it.

Scotland had large amounts of coal underground. It was mined in Midlothian, Fife, Ayrshire and the Glasgow area. In other parts of Scotland, people used wood to heat their homes. This was because there was a lot of it and it was easy to find.

By 1700, much of the wood had been used and people needed to find other ways of heating their homes. They began to buy coal. To supply the coal, the miners had to open more mines or dig even deeper into the ground. When they reached a coal-seam, they dug their way along the seam to get as much coal as they could.

The miners had to dig the coal from the seam using very simple tools. The coal then had to be carried to the surface using a system of ladders. This was very dangerous work. The deeper the mine was, the bigger the problems were.

In the west of Scotland the mines were very deep and miners had to use expensive machinery there. It was very rare to see women working in these mines. In the East, the mines were not so deep and they employed lots of women to do the work.

Young children worked in nearly all the mines in Scotland.

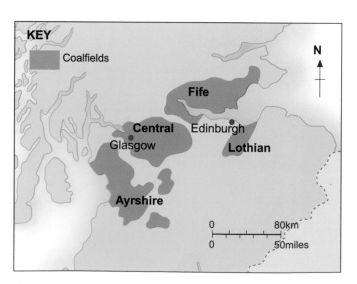

This map shows where coal is found in Scotland.

This drawing shows what a coal-mine was like in the early 1800s.

Digging Coal

Hewers had to work on their knees.
This drawing was made in 1842.

The coal had to be dug from a coal-face. The person who did this job was called a hewer. Because a hewer had to be very strong, this job was always done by men.

The hewer used a variety of tools to help him cut the coal. These included a pick, a hammer, chisels and a shovel. The hewer used the pick to dig out chunks of coal or used his hammer to drive wedges into the coal-seam to split the coal.

Hewing was a very skilled job. The hewer had to be careful how he used his tools because a mistake could bring tons of coal crashing down on his head.

The hewers agreed how much coal they would cut. This was usually 4s. (shillings) worth (20p in today's money) a day. Anyone who took more than his share could be fined.

Miners used tools like these.

shovel

chisels

hammer

pickaxe

wedges

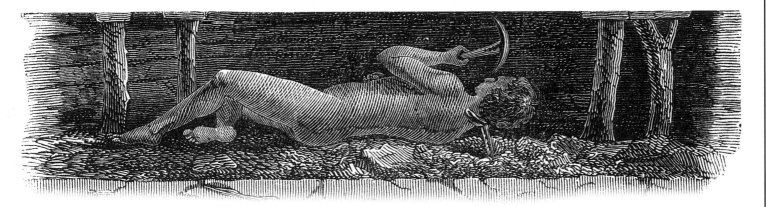

Another drawing from 1842 shows how hewers sometimes had to lie on their sides to work.

Hewers could cut more coal if they took their children to work with them down the mine. A ten-year-old boy was a 'quarter-man' and his father was allowed to dig an extra 1s. (5p) of coal a day.

At twelve years old, a boy became a 'half-man' and his father could then cut an extra 2s. (10p) of coal. A boy became a hewer himself when he reached the age of seventeen.

Sometimes the coal-seams were very narrow, perhaps only 50cm high, and this meant that only small men or young boys could be used to cut the coal. Hewers often had to work lying on their sides because there was not enough room to stand up.

Hewers always tried to cut large lumps of coal because they were paid more money for big pieces. They used wooden counters to record how much coal they sent to the surface. Hewers could earn more money than other workers at the time. Often, however, there was a shortage of hewers because it was such a difficult and dangerous job.

In 1842 the Government wrote a report about miners' lives. Some of the information that was collected for the report is shown, here, in green boxes.

At the time, George Reid was sixteen years old. This is how he described his job: 'I pick the coal at the coal-face, and I have done this for six years. The seam is 65cm high, and when I work I have to twist myself round. The men who work in this seam lie on their sides. It is horrible work and sore, too!

'No one ever goes up to eat their meals. Pieces of bread are taken down. Boys and girls drink the water in the mine but the men drink a small bottle of beer. I have often been hurt. A while ago I was off sick because the pick stuck into my side.

'Six of the family work with father in the pit. When work is good he can take home between £2 and £2.50 for the fortnight.'

To see in the dark, hewers in Scotland used a small lamp shaped like a jug. It was fixed to the miner's bonnet with a sharp hook.

9

Lifting Coal to the Surface

When the hewers had cut the coal, women carried it up to the surface. They were called bearers, and were often the wives and daughters of the hewers.

Some bearers started work at the age of six. They carried the coal in wicker baskets, called creels, along the mine shaft and up a series of steep ladders to the surface. This was very hard work. In places, they had to bend because of the low roof. In other places they had to walk through the water that had collected at the bottom of the mine.

The women went down the mine about three hours after the men had started digging. At the coal-face, two men loaded the creels and lifted them on to the backs of the bearers who had to carry them to the surface. Each load might weigh anything up to 65 kilos. Older women led the way along the dark tunnels, holding a candle in their teeth to light the path for the others behind.

Bearers carried heavy loads.

The women struggled to carry their heavy loads to the surface. Sometimes they even cried because their creel was so heavy. A bearer would make more than twenty trips from the coal-face to the surface in one day. Women would work like this for twelve or fourteen hours a day.

Bearers had to carry their loads up steep ladders to the surface.

Janet Cumming, an eleven-year-old coal bearer, describes her work:
'I work with my father and have done so for two years. Father starts at two o'clock in the morning and I go down with the women at five o'clock. I work until five at night. I work all night on Fridays and come up at midday on Saturdays.

'I carry coal from the face to the bottom of the pit shaft. The weight is usually 50 kilos and the distance between 50 and 80m. The roof is very low. I have to bend my back and legs, and the water often comes up to the calves of my legs. I do not like the work but my father makes me like it.'

Young children help their mother by pushing the cart while she pulls.

On the way to the surface, the bearers would pass a 'trapper'. The trapper was a young boy or girl whose job it was to open and close doors when bearers passed through. Trappers were usually eight years old but, sometimes, they were as young as six. They had to sit in the dark, wet and dangerous mine for at least ten hours at a time.

In some mines, boys and girls worked as 'putters' or 'drawers'. Their job was to fill wooden tubs or carts with coal and then to pull them to the bottom of the pit shaft. They wore harnesses and chains to pull the tubs full of coal. Usually, two young children worked together, one pulling the tub while the other pushed with both hands at the back.

A drawing from 1842 shows a trapper opening a door to let a cart through.

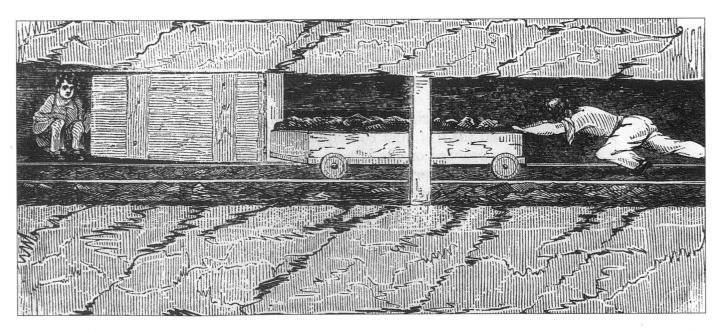

The Dangers of Working in a Mine

Working in a coal-mine was a dangerous job. Miners risked death every time they went underground. As mines went deeper into the ground, they became more dangerous.

EXPLOSION

Explosion was one of the biggest dangers in the mines. The candle on a miner's helmet, or even a spark caused by his pick hitting the coal-face, could easily ignite coal-dust or a gas called fire-damp. An explosion could kill a large number of miners at one time. In 1877, an explosion at the Blantyre Colliery near Glasgow killed over 200 miners.

To test for gas, a young boy was covered with wet sacks, and was sent along the mine seams with a lighted candle on the end of a long stick. This was a very dangerous job because the gas was likely to explode.

In most Scottish pits, a miner checked any dangerous areas with a Davy safety lamp before the day's work began.

POISONOUS GAS

Sometimes, gas did not explode. A gas, called choke-damp, suffocated the miners to death. The miners took canaries down the mine to warn them if choke-damp was there. If the birds stopped singing, the miners knew there was gas.

To stop the build-up of gases, better ventilation was needed. Ventilation meant taking the old air out and replacing it with fresh air. A fire was lit at the bottom of the pit to suck air into the pit.

This engraving shows a miner testing for fire-damp, which has exploded. Young boys often did this job.

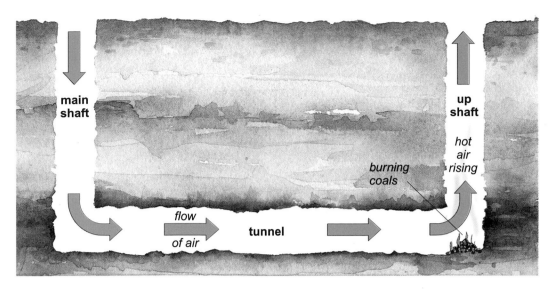

main shaft

up shaft

hot air rising

burning coals

flow of air

tunnel

Ventilating the coal-mines. The fire at the bottom of the pit drew fresh air deep into the mine. The trap doors (see middle left picture) made the air go everywhere in the mine and helped to stop the build-up of gases.

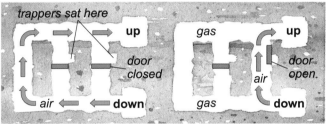

trappers sat here

up

door closed

air

down

gas

up

door open.

air

gas

down

ROOF-FALLS

Miners could be crushed to death if the roof of the mine fell on top of them. Alexander Gray's brother was killed when 'a piece of roof fell upon his head and he died instantly.'

Carrying heavy loads of coal was dangerous. The bearers might fall off the ladders when they got tired. They were also in danger of coal falling on their heads as they climbed the ladders to the surface. There was the chance that a lump of coal would fall out of a basket and land on the bearer coming up the ladder behind.

FLOODING

Flooding was another problem the miners had to face. The deeper the mine was, the more likely it was to flood.

Alexander Gray, aged ten, describes his attempts to pump out water from the mine in 1842:
'I pump out the water at the bottom of the pit. I have to pump fast or the water would cover me. I had to run away a few weeks ago because the water came up so fast that I could not pump at all. The miners had to leave the pit.'

Later, steam-engines were used to pump water out of the pits but they were expensive and most mine-owners could not afford to buy them.

This drawing from 1842 shows one of the dangers for coal bearers.

13

Moving Coal to the Factory

Coal is heavy, so it was difficult to move it from the mine to the nearest factory or town. Roads in 1842 were usually very bad. Coal was carried in small carts, which held less than one ton in weight. Sometimes coal was carried by pack-horse.

Moving coal by road was very slow and expensive. A ton of coal cost only 5s. (25p) at the mine. It cost 1s. (5p) to move one ton of coal one mile. This meant that, after moving the coal five miles from the pit, the price of the coal had doubled!

Mine-owners tried to find cheaper ways of moving their coal. Some of them laid rails to make wagon-ways. At first, these rails were made of wood. Later, they were made from solid iron. Some wagon-ways were built on a slope and the wagon just rolled down the hill. More often, the wagons were pulled by horses. Young boys were put in charge of the horses and it was their job to pull on the brake when they wanted the wagon to slow down or stop.

Horses pulled carts of coal along wagon-ways.

Wagon-ways became common around coal-mines in Central Scotland. The most famous wagon-way was built by the Duke of Pentland to carry coal from Kilmarnock to Troon. The coal was then shipped to Ireland. This wagon-way was one of the biggest ever built in Scotland and cost nearly £50,000. It also carried timber, grain and even people.

Many other wagon-ways were built to link the coalfields with the nearest canal. The easiest and cheapest way to transport heavy goods like coal was to send them by barge on a river or canal. New canals were built to connect the coalfields in Central Scotland with both Glasgow and Edinburgh. This made it easier and cheaper for the people in the cities to buy coal, so a lot more coal was sold.

Four canals were used to carry coal to the factories and the cities. These were the Forth and Clyde Canal, the Monkland Canal, the Glasgow, Paisley and Johnstone Canal and the Edinburgh and Glasgow Union Canal.

The opening of the Glasgow and Garnkirk Railway in 1831.

In 1826, a new railway joined Kirkintilloch to the Monkland Canal. At first, the railway used horses but, after 1832, it used steam-locomotives to pull the coal trucks. This railway made a lot of money so mine-owners and businessmen built more railways.

The Glasgow and Garnkirk Railway cut the cost of moving coal to Glasgow from 3s. 6d. (18p) to 1s. 3d. (7p) per ton. This made coal cheaper to buy. By 1836, it carried 140,000 tons of coal a year.

By the 1840s, a whole network of railways covered Central Scotland.

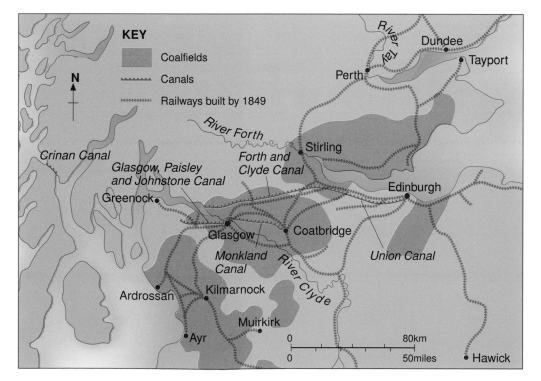

KEY

- Coalfields
- .... Canals
- ++++++ Railways built by 1849

These canals and railways were built mainly for carrying coal to the larger towns of Central Scotland.

Making Iron

Molten iron pours out of the furnace and runs into a mould.

To make iron, rocks called 'ironstone' or 'iron ore' had to be heated in a special furnace. When they reached a very high temperature, the iron in the rocks melted and ran out. This work was called 'smelting'. When all the iron had melted, it was allowed to pour out of the furnace. It ran along grooves in the ground where it cooled and went hard to form iron bars which were called 'pigs'.

'Pig iron' was not good enough to make things. It had to be melted again and was poured into moulds (or casts) to make 'cast iron' objects like stoves or grates. These were very heavy and broke very easily.

Wrought iron was far stronger and could be bent into all sorts of shapes. Pig iron was turned into wrought iron by heating it until it was red hot and then shaping it by hitting it with a hammer. This was a very skilled job. Of course, this extra work meant that wrought iron was more expensive than cast iron.

In 1783, Henry Cort discovered a new way to make wrought iron, which he called the 'puddling process'. Iron bars were heated in a 'puddling furnace' until they melted. Then, the metal was stirred by a 'puddler' until it became pure. The puddler had to use his skill to judge when the metal was ready.

The flames from ordinary wood and coal are not hot enough to melt iron. For hundreds of years, people used charcoal to smelt iron. Charcoal is made from wood. Many of the forests in Britain were cut down to make charcoal.

Ironworks were built at Invergarry in the Highlands and Bonawe in the north of Strathclyde, because there was plenty of wood there to make charcoal. It was easier to bring the ironstone to the Highlands than to take the charcoal to the Lowlands. Things changed after all the Highland forests were burned.

Just at this time, Abraham Darby discovered how to use coke to smelt ironstone. Coke was made from coal, so the iron-making industry moved to the coalfields. Ironstone was often found near coalfields as well.

For a long time, the Carron Ironworks at Falkirk were the biggest in Scotland. Its owners chose Carron because they had found plenty of coal and ironstone there and it was close to the River Forth. They could move their products by boat.

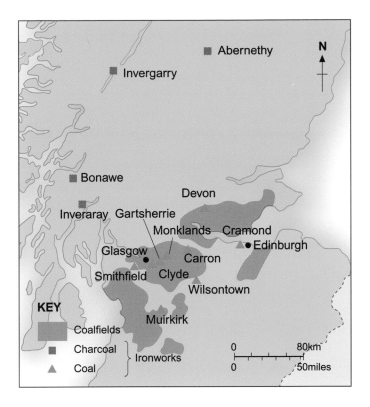

New ironworks opened up beside coalfields.

In 1828, however, James Neilson from Glasgow invented the 'hot blast furnace'. It reached a temperature of 300°C and produced three times more iron than an ordinary furnace. The new furnace made top-quality iron using 'blackband ironstone', which was a mixture of coal and ironstone. There were large amounts of blackband ironstone in Central Scotland and the iron industry grew very quickly there.

The Carron Ironworks was famous for a special cannon it made, called the carronade. It was a short gun which fired a heavy cannon-ball. It was used on the Royal Navy's ships, as this drawing shows, and by the army.

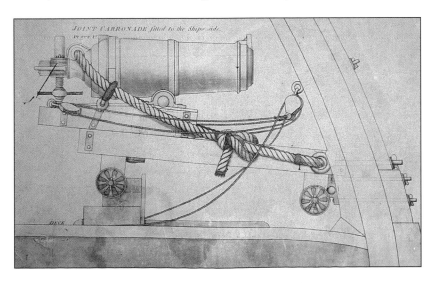

Working in a Foundry

Boys worked in the iron industry. Some started work when they were ten years old.

At the blast furnaces, where they made pig iron, boys made the moulds for the pigs. This work usually took them three hours. The moulds had to be ready for the moulding which took place at six o'clock in the morning and at six o'clock at night.

In iron foundries, boys aged thirteen or older made cast-iron items, like pots and pans. They, too, had to make moulds from sand. Then the boys had to carry molten metal to the moulds in big pots. This was very dangerous. They had to hang the pot from the middle of a long pole and two boys carried an end each.

Older boys had the job of pouring the metal into the moulds.

Other boys were employed in the puddling furnaces where pig iron was turned into wrought iron. Each puddler employed an 'underhand' to heat up the furnace for him. Usually, underhands started work when they were fourteen years old. In time, the puddler would allow his underhand to work the iron in the early stages of the puddling process.

Making pig iron. The bars of iron reminded the workers of a sow with her piglets. That was why the long channel for the iron was called a 'sow' and the little bars were called 'pigs'.

The puddler had to finish the work himself because puddling was a very skilled job. It was also very hot work because he had to keep the furnace door open so he could watch the metal to judge when it was ready. During this time, the underhand could have a rest for about twenty minutes. Then he had to start loading the furnace again while the puddler had his rest. The whole puddling process took about an hour and a half.

Some boys were employed in the work of hammering and rolling the iron into bars or rods. Ten-year-olds were employed to open furnace doors. Older boys were used to shape the red-hot iron rods by moving them through rollers.

Some of these boys were 'apprentices' which meant that they were learning to become skilled ironworkers. Others were sent to work to earn extra money for their family. A ten-year-old could earn 4s. (20p) a week while a fourteen-year-old puddler's underhand could take home 8s. (40p). To earn this, the boys had to work twelve hours a day. They were allowed to have two hours off for their meal breaks.

People at the time knew that there was a danger of boys being burned by red-hot metal. They did not think there was anything wrong about children working for so many hours each day. Instead, they were worried about boys learning bad habits from the older workers in the foundries, such as drinking, smoking and using bad language.

Taking iron out of a puddling furnace during the process of making wrought iron.

Increasing Demand for Coal and Iron

After 1820, more people in Scotland needed to buy coal. Farmers used coal to burn lime, which was then spread on their fields to produce better crops. Coal was also used in the making of lime mortar, which was needed to build houses in the new towns.

The population of Scotland was growing very quickly in the nineteenth century. More people were being born and they lived longer. Many of these people lived in cities. Glasgow had a population of 77,000 in 1801 but by 1851 this had increased to 329,000. Most of these people used coal to heat their homes.

This was also true of Edinburgh, which was known as 'Auld Reekie' because there was so much smoke from the city's chimneys. Even in country areas, where peat was becoming more difficult to find, people bought coal.

The Scottish engineer, William Murdoch, invented a system of gas lighting. This gas was made from coal. By the 1840s, nearly every major town in Britain used coal gas lighting. This meant much more coal was needed.

James Watt, another Scottish engineer, invented the steam-engine. By the 1840s, it was used by many industries but especially by the cotton factories around Glasgow. These steam-engines needed coal to power them.

Coal was also needed in many other industries, like glass-making, chemicals, sugar refining, and distilling. It was moved across Scotland on railways, which needed coal for the steam-locomotives. The great increase in Scottish railways after 1840

meant that demand for coal went up. At the same time, steamships became more common and they, too, needed coal.

COAL OUTPUT, Scotland (1750–1860)	
1750	500,000 (tons)
1808	1,800,000
1815	2,500,000
1854	7,400,000
1860	10,900,000

Railway locomotives and steamships were made from iron. To make these, more iron was needed. More coal was needed to make this iron. One writer said 'the furnaces of Airdrie and Coatbridge (Old Monklands) alone use as much coal in a year as the city of Glasgow, including all its factories.'

By 1850, Scottish ironworks used almost 2,500,000 tons of coal in a year, which was one-third of all coal mined in Scotland. The Gartsherrie ironworks used over 1,000 tons of coal every day.

Iron was used to make a lot of different things in the nineteenth century, such as bridges, steam-engines, water and gas pipes, cables, ploughs and nails, as well as pots and pans for the home.

IRON OUTPUT, Scotland (1806–1860)	
1806	22,000 (tons)
1823	24,000
1830	37,000
1840	241,000
1852	775,000
1860	1,017,000

By 1850, ships with iron hulls were cheaper than wooden ships and they were also stronger, lighter and lasted longer. Many of these ships were built in the shipyards on the Clyde.

The railways used iron for the track. The wagons and locomotives were also made from iron and they were usually built in Scotland. Much of the iron made in Scotland was sold to countries all over the world.

SS Persia had an iron hull and was made in Glasgow in 1855.

The Need for More Workers

Some Highlanders emigrated. This detail from Thomas Faed's painting *Last of the Clan*, 1865, shows friends and relatives left behind on the shore.

Before 1775, miners were treated like slaves. They could not leave their master's pit. After 1775, they were set free but other people still looked down on them. Some tradesmen and even some farm workers would not allow their daughters to marry miners.

Most people were put off by the dangers and hard work in the mines, so there was always a shortage of workers. This was about to change. Many Highlanders went to work in the mines because of the Highland Clearances. Landlords in the Highlands wanted more money than they could get from the poor Highlanders. Sheep farmers from the south offered the landlords high rents because they thought the Highlands would be perfect for sheep farming. In the Highland Clearances, landlords moved the people off the land to make way for sheep.

Many Highlanders were forced to emigrate to Canada, Australia or New Zealand. Most, however, chose to go to the growing industrial cities to find work in the factories and mines.

When the Highlanders went looking for work in the mines, they found they had competition from the Irish. From 1820, many Irish people moved to the Lowlands of Scotland to try to find work. The steamships provided them with a cheap and easy way of getting there.

In the 1840s, a potato famine had a terrible effect on Ireland. More than one million people starved to death. Many more Irish moved to Britain to find work. By 1851, almost 207,000 Irish immigrants lived in Scotland, with over 90,000 of them living in Glasgow.

The city could not cope with all these extra people and there was a shortage of jobs, houses, schools and churches. This caused a lot of bad feeling between the Scots and the Irish. The Irish usually stayed together in the poor areas of the city, where they felt they were safe.

Many Irish immigrants tried to get work in the local mines and ironworks. They were disliked by the Scots miners who saw them as foreigners trying to take over their jobs. Scottish miners said that the Irish were not real miners. They said the Irish were only labourers who had never worked in a coal-mine before and might cause accidents. Irish immigrants were also unpopular for religious reasons. Most Scots were Protestant and they disliked Irish Roman Catholics.

The mine-owners, unlike the miners, were pleased to see the Irish coming to Scotland. The Irish were willing to work for less money than the Scots. For this reason the Irish got all the jobs unless the Scots worked for less money as well. The mine-owners used the Irish to work when the Scots went on strike.

Many Irish people sailed to Scotland to find work.

New Industrial Towns

When new coal-mines and ironworks were opened, their owners needed to attract workers. These workers had to have homes nearby because they had to walk to work. Their employers had to build homes for them. As industry grew, towns had to grow as well.

The box below shows how the population of Old Monklands grew between 1794 and 1839. It also shows how the area produced more and more coal and iron.

	1794	1806	1839
Population	4,000	5,000	19,000
Iron production (in tons)	3,600	9,000	177,000
Coal production (in tons)	36,000	130,000	530,000

The owners were not really interested in building homes for their workers. They wanted to use their money to build up their businesses and to earn even more money for themselves. Besides, if a coal-mine ran out of coal, there would be no more need for the houses and the owner would have wasted his money! So, workers' houses were not well built.

This meant that the owner was not able to charge high rents. In fact, rents in Scotland were usually very low. Nobody would pay a lot of money for a poor house, and workers refused to pay higher rents for a better one. Low rents meant that owners did not have money to pay for repairs, and houses were allowed to get worse and worse.

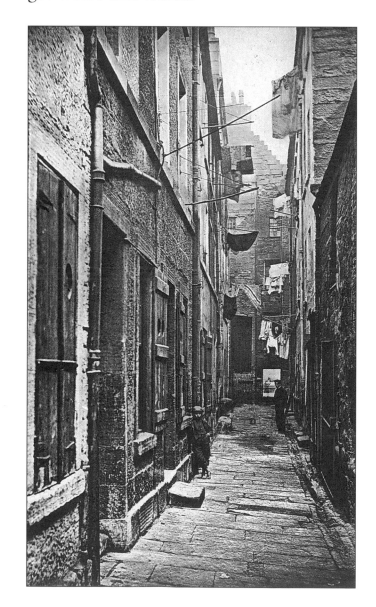

Houses in the slums were built very close to each other. This is in Glasgow in the 1860s.

There were no rules about how many rooms houses had to have, how many windows, or how big the rooms were to be. In fact, most miners' cottages had only one or two rooms where the whole family had to live.

There were no rules either about where houses could be built. They were usually built close to the workplace and all the dirt, dust and pollution it created.

A visitor to Coatbridge said, 'A coat of black smoke lies over everything.' Another visitor said, 'The groups of blast furnaces on all sides might be imagined to be blazing volcanoes.' During the day, people could see steam rising from the local canal where the water from the blast furnaces poured into it.

These towns had a poor water supply. People had to take their water from a pump in the street. Sometimes, the water was dirty and caused diseases.

There were no proper drains. Waste was thrown into a stream where people hoped it would be washed away. Other rubbish was thrown on to the 'midden' or rubbish heap. Toilet waste was kept and piled up until there was enough to sell to a local farmer who used it for manure.

It was hardly surprising that there were frequent outbreaks of diseases like cholera and typhus, which killed large numbers of people.

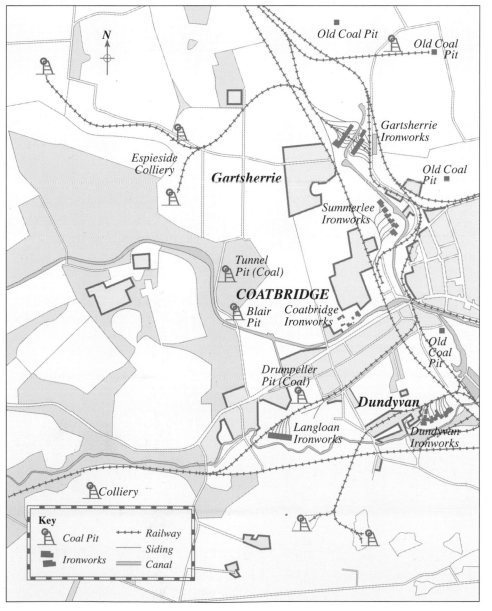

Towns like Coatbridge grew up beside coal pits and ironworks.

25

Housing

In the 1840s, families were much bigger than they are today. It was quite common for a family to have six, seven or eight children. The whole family had to crowd together into a house with only one or two rooms.

The rooms were quite small and there was not much space for furniture. There was a table, chairs and some stools, and one or two chests for clothes. The box beds were the biggest items in a room. They had solid walls on three sides and a door or curtains through which to get in and out. Quite often, the children had to sleep head-to-toe in these beds. Less fortunate children had to sleep on bedding on the floor. During the day, the bedding was put away beneath the box bed to leave the floor space clear.

There was always a shortage of houses in the new industrial towns. This caused even greater overcrowding. Families would take in lodgers, usually young men, because there was nowhere else for them to stay. In some places, visitors reported as many as fourteen lodgers living with a family in a two-roomed house!

This overcrowding was unhealthy. There was never enough fresh air in the small rooms. Illness and disease could spread quickly through all the members of a household.

A street of miners' houses in Stanburn.

The inside of a miner's house at Redding, near Falkirk.

Houses could not be kept tidy and clean. The number of people living in a house, and the fact that there was so much dirt in the air, made this an impossible task.

In coal-mining areas especially, women would be at work for most of the day. They could not be expected to cook and make a good job of cleaning and tidying the house as well.

Families kept animals in their houses. In addition to dogs and cats they often had hens and pigs, which were fed scraps of food. They got eggs from the hens and, when the pig was big and fat, they killed it and ate it. Of course, the dirt attracted mice and rats.

Visitors to these new towns all noticed how dirty the people were. There were no water taps in the houses, so people had to draw water from a well or a pump and carry it to their homes. Sometimes, they just took water from a river or stream and hoped that it was clean.

One visitor to a coal-mining village said that the people were all dirty but that they usually washed their faces when they came home from work. 'Sometimes,' he added, 'the children follow their example!'

Another visitor described the ragged and dirty clothes of the people and said that the skin of the children seemed 'perfectly innocent of water.'

The Power of the Mine-Owner

The mine-owner employed three men to control his mine and the lives of the miners.

He would use a manager to run the mine for him. The manager hired the miners and paid them for the coal they brought to the surface. This was an important job, and the manager was usually well paid, especially if the mine made a lot of money.

The mining oversman was in charge of the miners underground. He also had to check that the tunnels were safe for work.

The checksman had to check how much coal each miner brought to the surface. He also made sure it was good-quality coal and not ordinary stones. There were always arguments between the miners and the checksman about this.

Miners were usually only given a job for a year. If their work was not good or they were seen as troublemakers, they would not be kept on. In some places, the miners were only hired for a few weeks at a time.

All the miners had to follow a strict set of rules. Anyone who broke the rules was likely to be fined or even sacked.

Here are some rules taken from a coal-mine in Ayr:

The rich life of the mine-owners was paid for by the hard and dangerous work of the poor miners. This cartoon was published in the Punch magazine in 1843.

Any miner who joined a trade union had to pay a fine of £5.

Any miner who failed to finish a day's work would lose all his wages for that day.

Any miner who took away the tools of another miner was fined 2s. 6d. (about 13p).

Any miner who hit another miner was fined 2s. 6d. (about 13p), or 5s. (25p) if he had hit someone before.

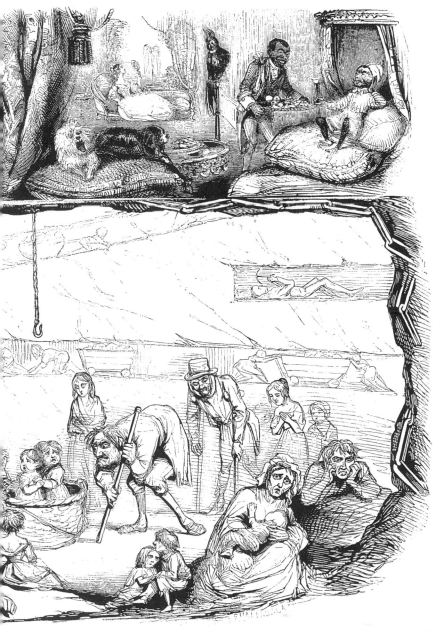

Once the manager had made a decision, the miners could not argue with him. Miners were not allowed to hold meetings to talk about their work and they were certainly not allowed to join a trade union.

The miners had to do what they were told because the mine-owner owned their houses. He often also paid for his miners' children to go to the local school. If a miner lost his job, he would lose his home as well and his children would have to leave school.

Mine-owners lived a life of luxury in large houses. They could afford to buy the best furniture. Their walls were covered with fine paintings. Servants did all their housework.

If a mine grew big enough, the owner could rent it to a coal or iron company, which would pay a lot of money to use the mine.

Mine-owners were important people in a town. They had a place on the town council. Local churches, schools and the poor all needed money from the rich mine-owners. They would not get money unless they did what the owners wanted. Sometimes, mine-owners might even be elected to parliament to make new laws.

The mine-owners' children would not work down the mines. They would go to private schools and enjoy all the privileges of being rich.

The Village Shop

In the 1840s, it was not easy for people to travel from place to place. Most workers had to walk. When new villages grew up, people needed local shops for their groceries.

The owners of mines and foundries spotted a chance to earn some extra money for themselves. They built the village shop and made their workers buy their groceries from it.

Sometimes, instead of giving the workers money in their fortnightly wage packets, their employers gave them tokens for their shops. This forced the workers to buy their groceries there, because no other shops would accept the tokens. When the workers went to their employers' shops, they discovered that everything there was much dearer than it was elsewhere.

The Government finally passed a law to stop employers doing this. The employers, however, found ways around the law. Wages were usually paid once every two weeks. Some employers paid their workers only once a month. This meant that workers were often very short of money before their next pay day.

The village shop in Dunaskin, Ayrshire, in the early 1900s. The building on the hill on the right is the village school.

This was just what the shop-owning employer wanted. He allowed his workers to take the groceries they needed, and he would take the money from their next wages. As might be expected, he took more than the goods were really worth. By doing this, he made sure that the workers would again run out of money before their next pay day.

The workers spent much of their money on alcohol, especially beer, gin and whisky. Visitors to the new coal and iron towns wrote about the many shops that sold alcohol and what a bad effect it had on the people. They blamed much of the dirt and misery of these places on the fact that the parents spent all their spare time drinking rather than keeping a good home. These visitors were very worried that children were not being looked after properly and were learning bad habits from adults.

One visitor was very pleased to announce that he had spoken to a miner who did not drink. The miner said that he had saved up so much money that he had been able to buy his own house!

Mr Tancred, who toured these new villages to write a report for the Government, described one visit:
'I remember the house of a workman where I found the wife in tears. There was hardly a piece of furniture in the house. The only seat was just a board supported by two big lumps of coal. The bed spaces and walls were totally bare. When I asked the poor woman about why her house was so poor, she blamed her husband's drinking for it.

'I was astonished to find out from his boss that he was a very skilled workman. I finally met the man at the store where he was trying to buy more whisky. He was making such a row that the manager had to throw him out and to bar the door afterwards.'

Many visitors were shocked to see how miners spent their spare time.

Health and Medicine

Dirty, overcrowded streets led to the spread of disease.

At this time, doctors did not know about germs and bacteria, which can give people diseases like cholera, small pox, typhus and scarlet fever. People died from these diseases because doctors did not know what caused them.

Doctors blamed dirt and overcrowding for the spread of disease. One doctor said that he often saw whole families where everyone was ill.

Doctors said that, if the houses were cleaned up, the people would be healthier. They compared the dirty houses and bad health of workers in towns with the clean houses and good health of farm workers. They noticed that farm workers usually lived twenty years longer than male coalminers. Hardly any miners lived to be more than fifty years old.

Doctors had also noticed how the miners' health got worse as they grew older. They did not think that miners' children were healthy in the first place. 'But,' they said, 'anyone could see the difference in these children after their first six months down a pit.'

After that, the doctors reported that the miners' children did not grow as quickly as children elsewhere. They also suffered breathing difficulties, had coughs and some of them lost an eye when the coal dust made it swell. The doctors blamed all of this on very young children being forced to work very hard for long hours underground. They also complained that these children did not have good food and regular mealtimes when they went underground.

Miners' wives usually lived longer than miners. The doctors decided that this was because they did not work down the mines for as many years as their husbands. Most miners' wives stopped underground work when their children were old enough to work there instead. The women who continued to work down the mines were harmed by it. One complained that her work underground was 'only horse work which ruins the women. It crushes their haunches [the tops of their legs], bends their ankles and makes them old women.'

The 'Black Spit' was a disease that killed many miners. It got its name because victims coughed up black mucus. They became weak and short of breath. The doctors knew about the effects of

Country children were bigger and heavier than miners' children.

the illness, but not how it was caused.

Doctors felt that perhaps the gunpowder used to blast coal caused the Black Spit, but they were not sure. One doctor even carried out an experiment on the lungs cut from a man who had died from Black Spit. He discovered that the man's lungs looked black like coal, and burned just like it as well!

Compared to working down a coalmine, children employed making iron had much safer jobs. Usually, they worked out-of-doors, or in open sheds. They did not start to work at such a young age, and they did not work for such long hours. Mealtimes were regular and, usually, someone brought a hot meal to the workplace for them. However, there were some reports that looking at red-hot molten metal sometimes affected their eyesight.

Accidents at Work

Accidents were common in coal-mines. Rocks could fall from the roof of the mine or women could drop coal while they were carrying it up the ladders to the surface. Sometimes people were injured when underground trucks collided with each other. A few people were even caught in the winding mechanism that pulled up baskets of coal in some mines.

In fact, accidental deaths were so common in coal-mines that no one bothered to find out why they happened.

Injuries in ironworks were not so common. The work was dangerous because of the fires and molten metal, but people were very careful. In fact, visitors commented that boys were injured only occasionally, usually by standing on some red-hot metal.

Doctors found it difficult to treat injuries. Anaesthetics, which prevent a patient feeling pain, had not been discovered and this meant that doctors had no way of reducing pain. It also meant that the patients were wide awake during surgery. If the doctor had to remove a mangled arm or leg, he had to tie the patient to the table while he operated.

Some doctors knocked patients out by hitting them. Some patients were just given a piece of wood to bite on while the doctors operated. Others were given whisky to make them unaware of what was happening. Whisky, however, caused medical problems which could kill the patients.

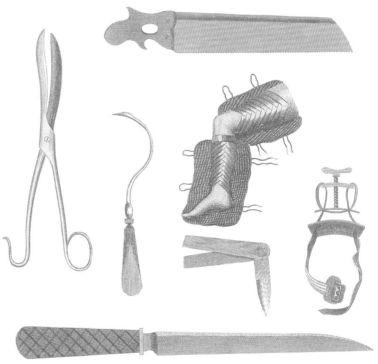

Surgeons used tools like these for operating on and treating patients.

The doctors tried to work as quickly as possible. Sometimes, they made mistakes because they were rushing their work.

Doctors thought that their problems were over when Professor James Young Simpson of Edinburgh University discovered chloroform. Patients could be sent to sleep by breathing in the chloroform and doctors could then take time to operate carefully.

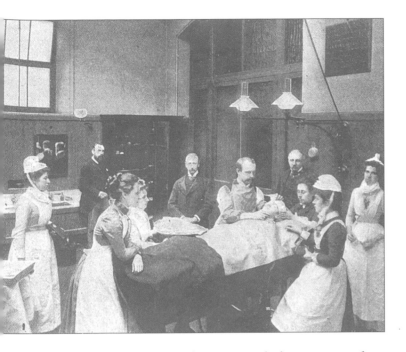

After anaesthetics were discovered, doctors could take time to operate. This operation took place in about 1890.

Doctors soon discovered, however, that even more patients died than before. This was because doctors did not know about germs. They did not know about how important it is to keep everything spotlessly clean. Doctors would operate on kitchen tables, or even on the ground. Dirt and germs could get into a wound very easily. This would cause blood poisoning which could kill the patient.

A French doctor, Louis Pasteur, discovered germs. Professor Joseph Lister, who worked in Scotland, found that a substance called carbolic would kill most germs. Doctors would spray carbolic over their patients while they operated. This discovery meant that operations had to be carried out in hospitals. Trained nurses gave patients much better medical attention than their families

could give them at home. The number of people recovering from surgery increased very quickly.

Doctors had to be paid by their patients. This meant that poor people did not call for the doctor unless they were seriously ill. As a result, they often waited too long before they sent for a doctor. The doctor would arrive to find that it was too late to save his patient.

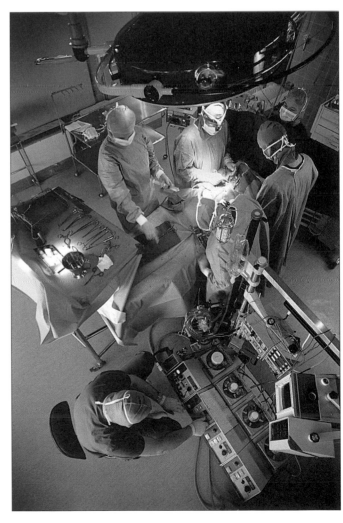

Compare this picture of a modern operation with the photograph above taken one hundred years ago.

Education

Scotland had been very proud of its education system. Every parish in Scotland had a parish school and all of the boys and some of the girls were taught to read, write and do arithmetic.

The parents of pupils were expected to pay the teacher for their lessons but the church usually paid for the lessons of the poor. It cost 3d. (about 1p) a week to learn how to read and 4d. a week for writing or for arithmetic lessons. Extra schools were built where there were too many pupils for one school or where the parish school was too far away.

In 1842, there was no law that made boys and girls go to school every day.

Most parents sent their children to school. This changed because of the new industries.

The old schools could not take the extra pupils who arrived when a village or town suddenly grew bigger. One teacher found that he had 140 pupils in a school that was big enough for only fifty. He had to make his reading class stand up so his other pupils would have room to do their writing.

Those children who went to school stopped attending when they went to work. Miners' children had less education because they started work at a much younger age than other children.

The classroom of a parish school.

Schools taught reading, writing and arithmetic. This school, photographed in the 1850s, was held in a church.

wages to pay for lessons. The children did not have to go, so many of them did not bother.

In many places, the schoolmaster organized night classes to teach working children. Usually, these classes were for pupils who had already learned to read. The schoolmaster taught them writing and arithmetic.

These night schools were not as successful as the schoolmasters hoped. Most of the children were so tired from their day's work that they could not pay proper attention to their lessons. Some of the children had to work overtime, which meant they missed their lessons. They found it very hard to catch up.

Visitors to the new towns were very worried about the lack of education for the children. Almost everyone agreed that the children needed to go to school. In 1872, an Education Act made it the law that every child should go to school until the age of thirteen.

Few of them ever went back to school. They did not like to be in classes with other children who were younger than them, but ahead of them in their lessons.

Children were usually older before they started work in the ironworks. This meant that they had received some education. Indeed, some ironworks would only employ boys who had learned to read and write properly.

Some mine-owners tried to make their workers send their children to school. They took 2d. a week from miners'

Changing the Mines

In 1840, Parliament set up a committee to find out about working conditions in mines and ironworks. It spent two years visiting many areas of Britain, talking to people who worked there. The committee then produced a report.

People were shocked by the Coal Commission Report of 1842. They did not know the mines were so dreadful. Here are some of the things children said:

'I work twelve hours a day. I have often been hurt. I had my ankle cut open and was off work for six weeks.'
Ann Smith, coal putter.

'I have to carry my load up four ladders until I get to the pit bottom. I have to make twenty journeys to fill five tubs of coal. I have had the strap when I don't work hard enough.'
Ellison Jack, coal bearer.

'My two sisters were badly crushed by stones falling from the roof, their insides were forced out and their legs were broken.'
Robert Robinson, coalminer.

When people read the 1842 Report and found out about the terrible conditions, they demanded a change in the law. A new law, the 1842 Mines Act, stopped all girls, women and boys under the age of ten working underground. The Government sent inspectors to check that the mine-owners were obeying the law.

NOTICE.

NO FEMALES

Permitted, on any account, to work under ground at this Colliery; and all such is **STRICTLY PROHIBITED**, by Orders from His Grace the Duke of Hamilton.

JOHN JOHNSTON, Overseer.

REDDING COLLIERY, 4 March 1845.

After the law changed in 1842, this poster was put up at mines.

A drawing of a Fifeshire putter from 1842.

Some people were angry about the new law. Mine-owners said the report was not fair because the children had not told the truth. A few women complained that they had lost their jobs and had no other way to earn money.

The Government made more new laws about working conditions in mines:

1855 ventilation in mines had to be improved;

1860 boys under twelve were no longer allowed to work in the mines unless they could read and write;

1862 mines with only one shaft were closed;

1872 managers had to have a certificate to show that they could do their job properly.

Miners set up trade unions to fight for more changes. Some miners were elected to parliament, where they tried to make more new laws about mines. The Scottish miners' leader Keir Hardie became the first leader of the Labour Party.

As more coal was needed and mines went deeper underground, there was a need for new machinery. This machinery changed coal-mines. Steam-engines were used to lift coal to the surface and to lower miners down the pit. They were also used to pump water out of it. After 1860, steam-driven fans were used to suck fresh air into the mine.

Wagon-ways were laid underground to move the coal from the coal-face to the shaft. The wagons were pulled along the rails by ponies.

The discovery of electricity solved many problems in the pit. Electricity provided light for the miners. Electric cutting and digging machinery was also invented. Huge electric motors were used to pull wagons underground. However, small mines could not afford to buy this expensive machinery. They still used the old ways.

Machinery changed the mines and made them safer. They could also go much deeper.

Children Working Today

Today, children in Britain are not allowed to leave school and start work until they are over sixteen years old. While they are under sixteen, they are expected to go to school every week-day during the school term.

Pupils are not expected to work for long hours at school. They are usually there for just six hours a day. This includes time for breaks and lunch. There might, perhaps, be an extra hour of homework after school. No one is expected to be at school for ten to twelve hours a day and no one has to go to school during the night. In the past, children were expected to work for

These young children work in a brick storage yard in Cambodia, South East Asia.

these long hours and then to go to school afterwards.

When they are older, some of today's pupils are allowed to start part-time work for a few hours a day. There are laws to make sure that they do not work too long. These laws also make sure that they do not work in places that are dangerous, like coal-mines or foundries. Employers who break these laws can be taken to court and fined a lot of money.

British laws do not apply to other countries in the world. In some Third World countries, children are being forced to work down mines. They are made to do jobs that British children have not been allowed to do for over one hundred years.

In Africa, South America, India and many other parts of the world, children are being forced to work long hours making charcoal and coke for the iron industry.

Many children are being injured or are becoming ill because of their work, but they cannot afford doctors and medicine to help them. Most of them are forced to work because of poverty. Their parents need the money the children earn to keep their families alive. The wages the children are paid are very low, but it is enough to make the difference between eating and starving. In some countries, the parents are so poor that they have to sell their children as slaves.

Children are still forced to work in dangerous mines. This boy is a coalminer in Colombia in South America.

Organizations like the United Nations are trying to stop slavery. They are finding it very difficult to do this in poor countries where parents cannot afford to look after their children. Parents and slave-owners tell lies to hide what is really happening.

One hundred and fifty years ago many British children led miserable lives working in the coal and iron industries.

Today, in different parts of the world, children are still living miserable lives.

Glossary

Barge A flat-bottomed boat used for moving heavy goods along canals and rivers.

Bearer A woman who carried coal on her back in the mines.

Black Spit A lung disease that killed many miners.

Canals Man-made rivers. Barges were used to move coal and iron along canals.

Cast iron Iron that has been shaped in a mould.

Charcoal Fuel made from burnt wood.

Coal-face The part of a mine where coal is found and dug out.

Coalfield An area where coal is found.

Committee A small group of people chosen to do a job for everyone else.

Creels Wicker baskets in which coal was carried in the mines.

Davy Lamp A safety lamp designed in 1815 by Sir Humphry Davy for use in mines. The flame of the lamp was surrounded by very fine wire netting (gauze) to prevent it causing an explosion of gas.

Drawer A child who pulled tubs of coal underground.

Emigrate To leave one's native country to live in another country.

Foundry A place where iron is made.

Furnace A very hot oven used to smelt iron.

Hewer A man who cut coal underground.

Immigrant A person who comes to live in a country that is not his or her native country.

Law Rules made by the Government.

Manager A man whose job it was to look after a coal-mine for its owner.

Overtime Working more hours than normal.

Pack-horse A horse that carried goods in bags, or packs, on its back.

Parish A local area, which had its own church and school.

Peat The remains of plants that have been lying underground for millions of years. For centuries, peat has been dug up and used as fuel.

Pig iron Bars of rough iron.

Protestants Christians who do not follow the ideas taught by the Pope in Rome and who set up their own Church.

Puddler A man who stirs molten iron in a puddling furnace.

Puddling furnace A furnace in which pig iron is melted and stirred to form wrought iron.

Putter A child who pushed tubs of coal underground.

Roman Catholics Christians who accept the religious ideas followed and taught by the Pope in Rome.

Seam A layer of coal underground.

Smelting Heating iron ore until the metal runs out of the rock.

Trade union A group of workers who join together to try to get better working conditions and pay.

Tradesmen People who buy and sell goods.

Trapper A child who opened and closed ventilation doors in the mines.

Ventilation Creating a draught to replace old, stale air and gases with fresh air.

Wagon-ways Wooden or iron rails along which carts could be pulled by horses or steam-engines.

Wrought iron Iron that has been shaped and strengthened by hitting it with a hammer.

A map of Scotland, including some
places mentioned in the text.

Key

Mountains

● Towns/cities

0   80km

0   50miles

SHETLAND

ORKNEY

*N O R T H
S E A*

LEWIS

NORTH UIST

BENBECULA

SOUTH UIST

BARRA

RAASAY

SKYE

CANNA

RUM

EIGG

COLL

TIREE

ULVA   MULL

*A T L A N T I C
O C E A N*

JURA

ISLAY

ARRAN

● Invergarry

S C O T L A N D

● Aberdeen

● Bonawe

● Dundee

● Perth

Stirling

● Kirkcaldy

Falkirk
●

Greenock
●

Glasgow
●

● Edinburgh

● Newtongrange

Paisley
●

● Coatbridge

● Kilmarnock

● Ayr

Patna
●

I R E L A N D

E N G L A N D

Further Information

Places to visit

Dunaskin Heritage Centre, Patna, Ayrshire KA6 7JF
Telephone: 01292 531144
This includes the ironworks established at Dunaskin in the 1840s, a restored ironworker's cottage and remains of coalminers' housing, the village store, school, church and railway station, and ironworking and coalmining equipment.

Scottish Mining Museum, Lady Victoria Colliery, Newtongrange, Midlothian EH22 4QN
Telephone: 0131 663 7519
Including the Lady Victoria Colliery, established in the late nineteenth century, and a large collection of coalmining equipment.

Summerlee Heritage Trust, West Canal Street, Coatbridge ML5 1QD
Telephone: 01236 431261
Collections and reconstructions at Summerlee show Scotland's social and industrial history, focusing on ironworking and engineering, and including reconstructions of part of a coal-mine and miners' housing. Canals and railways also feature.

BBC Education Scotland has produced the following units of programmes on the Industrial Revolution:

For TV: *Children of Coal and Iron* in *Around Scotland* (transmission, Autumn 1995).
For radio: *People in the Past* in *Scottish Resources: 10-12* (transmission, Spring 1996).

A poster pack is also available. Information on ordering this and print support materials is available from:
BBC Education Scotland, Room 305, 5 Queen Street, Edinburgh EH2 1JF.
Telephone: 0131 469 4262.

Index